Prayers of Creation

Ray Simpson

God of life, you summon the day to dawn
and call us to create with you.

You are the Rock from which all earth is fashioned.
You are the Food from which all souls are fed.
You are the Force from which all power lines travel.
You are the Source who is creation's head.

You are the Heart from which all hearts are beating.
You are the Mind from which come thoughts and dreams.
You are the Eye from which comes all our seeing.
You are the Gift from whom all mercy streams.

You are the Ache from which comes all our longing.
You are the Wound in which we bear our pain.
You are the Wind by which all souls go winging.
You are the One from whom flows life again.

I arise today in the goodness of creation.
I arise today in the verdure of the fertile ground.
I arise today in the promise of the rising seed.

Glad Bringer of brightness,
day's blessing, rainbow's embrace,
teach our hearts to open as the buds open
and to welcome in your grace.
Teach us to dance with the playful clouds
and to laugh with sun's smile on our face.
The earth is yours, may it bring forth its produce.
The birds are yours, may they bring forth their songs,
our work is yours, may it bring forth its yield.

Glorious Source, we give you greeting!
Let Sister Earth and Brother Sun praise you.
Let the fields and the forests praise you.
Let the birds and the beasts praise you.
Let everything that has breath praise you,
Mother and Father of all that has being.

High-borne eagles and nesting birds,
be one with God's friends on earth.

Speckled trout and mountain deer,
speak, without words, God's praise.

Snarling wolf and savage boar,
lie down at sainted feet.

Serpents of fear and fierce desire,
uncoil and concede defeat.

Creatures tame and creatures wild,
show to us a living God.

We give you thanks for great moments of grace
in the evolution of the cosmos:
for the death of a star which brought to birth
planet Earth;
for the appearance of life forms;
for the emergence of minerals, vegetables, and animals;
for the cooperation, and not just the competition,
between all that lives.

We give thanks for the moments of grace
in the life of a person:
for the power of attraction and the wonder of a birth;
for the human person,
endowed with conscience, awe, and intelligence,
a co-creator with you.

Glory to the Birther, glory to the Son, glory to the Spirit
making creation one.

Creator of our land,
our earth, the trees,
the animals, and humans—
all is for your honor.

You pulled the continents out of the sea;
out of wet mud you have fashioned a wonderful world,
and what beautiful men and women!

The grace of your creation is like a cool day
between rainy seasons.
We drink in your creation with our eyes and with our ears.
How strong, good, and sure your earth smells—
and everything that grows there.

We drink in your creation and cannot get enough of it,
but we forget the evil we have done.
Tear us away from our sins.
This wonderful world fades,
and one day our eyes snap shut.
Then all that is not from you is over and dead.

Let the people say with joy
that you are the Lord.

Echoes a prayer from Ashanti, Ghana.

Creator, make us coworkers with you,
that the earth and all who live upon it
may reap a full harvest.

Show us how to reflect your rhythms
in our life and work
and to conserve the world's rich resources.

Help us to give all creatures their due respect,
to tend cattle and crops with care.

Guide science along wise and considerate ways,
that we may fashion agriculture that truly enhances,
and that we may sustain a vibrant environment.

Generosity of God,
spilling over into creation,
we bless you for flowers and their wealth of beauty, for
creatures and their glorious variety,
for seas and seasons and scents.

May we, too, reflect something of your
glorious generosity.

We pray for the well-being of the creation,
the healthiness of the air,
the richness of the earth,
the beauty of the world.

Creator and Savior,
we have exploited earth for our selfish ends,
turned our backs on the cycles of life,
and forgotten we are your stewards.
Now soils become barren,
air and water become unclean,
species disappear,
and humans are diminished.

Forgive us, and make us worthy stewards.

Forgive us ...

for polluting waste dumped by rich nations on lands of the poor;
for the lust of the few to own and control life forms;
for the new colonialism of women, plants, and animals;
for turning your gifts of water and life itself into products for gain;
for turning the sowing of seed from a sacred duty into a crime;
for destruction of biodiversity.

Creator, we have raped and spoiled your world.
Forgive.
Savior, we have ignored your warnings to tend
your earth like a vineyard.
Forgive.
Sustainer, we have tried to live without you.
Forgive.

God of creation,
make us aware of your presence
in every cell of creation
and in every cell of our being.

May the forests continue to grow,
may the trees continue to breathe,
for they also serve who only stand and wait.

Dear Savior,
who restored unity between earth and heaven,
teach us to care for your earth,
and to be good stewards of all that is in it.
May we learn how to live in harmony with your laws.

Bless the soil on which we live, work,
and make community.
May it bring forth goodness to nourish and renew all
who share it.

Great Spirit, whose breath is felt in the soft breeze,
may we cherish the earth.
May we provide for those who can neither sow nor
reap because human ills have drained them.

Father, bless the pet,
also bless the vet.
Savior, bless the flock,
also bless the cock.
Spirit, bless the horse,
also bless my course.

God of creation,
your Spirit brooded over the chaos
and brought a universe to birth;
you rejoiced at each day of creation,
delighting in its goodness before the hosts of heaven.
You breathed your life into all creatures
and your Spirit into us,
and so made a marriage of heaven and earth.
May we treasure our kinship with all creation
which finds its communion in you.

You who put beam in moon and sun,
you who put fish in stream and sea,
you who put food in ear and herd,
send your blessing up to me.
Bring forth the warmth, the tears, the laughter,
from our repressed and frozen ground.
Bring forth loving, healing, forgiving,
to our fretting, festering wound.

Spring

O Monarch of the Tree of Life,
may the blossoms bring forth the sweetest fruit,
may the birds sing out the highest praise,
may your Spirit's gentle breath cover all.

After the Carmina Gadelica.

Summer

God of the rising green,
God of the sweeping blue,
God of the long, bright day,
may I, too, give glory to you.

The sun rides high and long,
a sign of blessing from our God.
All that breathes cries "Yes!"
We say yes to the eternal Sun.

Farewell season of sowing and hidden striving,
now toil will bear its fruit.
Beauty, once hidden,
will come forth like a bride.

Welcome, season of growth and friendship,
season of activity, and celebration.
May ardor, vigor, and chivalrous love
flow strongly in our veins.
May holy heroes shine forth.

Autumn

Harvester God, as autumn light ripens the grain,
ripen too our souls.
As brown leaves fall and sheaves are stored,
help us to leave behind summer's ways,
and go forward in deepening compassion,
thankful to heaven.

The sheaves and the green leaves fall.
Generous be our hearts,
open be our hands,
justice be our benchmark,
thanksgiving be our call.

For the sake of your great giving,
O Christ who was ground like flour,
   our Bread of Life,
feed and nourish us evermore.

The seed is Christ's, the granary is Christ's.
In the granary of God may we be gathered.
The sea is Christ's, the fishes are Christ's.
In the nets of God may we all meet.

Winter

Christ at the yearly turning,
Christ at every bend,
Christ at each beginning,
Christ at every end.

Christ in dark's deep shadows,
Christ in shades of death,
Christ in primeval history,
Christ in wintry earth.

We arise today
in the simplicity of the bare soil,
in the strength of the fierce elements,
in the deep formation of winter.

Stripped of inessentials we stand, rooted in you.
In the anticipation of gathering strength,
you sustain our well-being.
In the humility of the bare earth,
we invite you to do your work in us.

Craftsperson of the heavens,
you have stretched out above us a canopy of stars
which are signs of hope renewed in darkest times.

Brightener of the night,
open to us the treasures of darkness—
its deepest wisdom
and its healing power.

May our eyes be open to see your hand in nature.
May our hands be open to cherish your gifts
in the material things around.
May we learn how to live in harmony with your laws.
Bless the soil on which we live,
work, and make community.
May it bring forth goodness
to nourish and renew all who share it.

Star Kindler and Weaver of wonder,
as winter stars light up the darkness of night,
reveal to us fresh sources of hope.

In the chill of wintry wind,
in the depths of uncertain thoughts,
sing to us the story of the universe,
visit us as Savior of our being.

Life-giver,
bring buds to flower,
bring rain to the earth,
bring songs to our hearts.

Renewer,
may gardens become green,
may beauty emerge,
may dreams come to pass.

We bless you, Lord,
for the beauty of the trees,
the softness of the air,
the fragrance of the grass.

We bless you, Lord,
for the soaring of the skies,
the rhythms of the earth,
the stillness of the night.

We bless you, Lord,
for the freshness of the morning,
the dewdrops on the flower,
for the twinkling of the stars.

We bless you, Lord,
for the taste of good food,
the trail of the sun,
and the life that never goes away.

Chief Dan George

In dependence on the God of life,
may we cherish the precious earth,
the earth of the God of life,
the earth of the Christ of love,
the earth of the Spirit Holy.
In dependence on the God of life,
may the earth be our bed of hope.

This we know, the earth does not belong to us.
The earth is God's and so are all people.
This we know, we did not weave the web of life.
The earth is God's, and so is all that breathes on it.
Whatever befalls the earth
befalls the sons and daughters of the earth.
The earth is God's, and so we will serve it.

May I be real, like the elements.
May I be true, like the fire.
May I be free, like the wind.
May the love that is within me flow, like water,
and may I not forget the fifth element, the flowers.
Dear God, give me fragrance in my relationships.

Creator, you caused the earth to bring forth the Savior.
Spirit, come now and renew the face of the earth.
All that grows on it, all who live on it.

We give you thanks
because earth's life and fruitfulness flow from you,
and all times and seasons reflect your laws.
We give you thanks
because you created the world in love,
you redeemed the world through love,
you maintain the world by your love.
Help us to give our love to you.

God, bless to us our bodies,
God, bless to us our souls,
God, bless to us our living,
God, bless to us our goals.

Thank you,
Creator of the world,
for the music and medicine of flowers
which give us a scent of heaven upon earth,
and for their vases which enable them to give their best.

Earthmaker God, as the hand is made for holding and
the eyes for seeing,
you have fashioned me for joy.
Grant me your vision that I may find it everywhere—

in the sunlit faces of our world,
in the wildflower's beauty, in the lark's melody,
in a child's smile, a mother's love,
in the face of a steadfast man.

Our society is ever-restless,
always craving one more thing to do,
seeking happiness through more and more possessions.

Teach us to be at peace with what we have.
To embrace what we have given and received;
to know that enough is enough,
until our strivings cease
and we rest content in you alone.

God bless the earth that is beneath us,
the sky that is above us,
the life that lies before us,
your image deep within us.

Echoes a traditional Scottish blessing.

After creation God rested.
We give back our lives to you.

Thank you for your love for us, strong and nurturing.
We give back our lives to you.

Thank you for our minds and bodies.
We give back our lives to you.

Thank you for the past day.
We give back our lives to you.

May the blessing of the rain be on us,
the sweet soft rain.
May it fall upon our spirits
so that all the little flowers may spring up
and shed their sweetness on the air.
May the blessing of the great rains be upon us
that they beat upon our spirits and wash them
fair and clean,
and leave there many a shining pool
where the blue of heaven shines,
and sometimes a star.

Echoes a traditional Irish blessing.

Blest be all creation
and all that has life.
Blest be the earth;
may it uplift our bed tonight.
Blest be the fire,
may it glow in us tonight.
Blest be the water,
may it bathe our being tonight.
Blest be the air,
may it make our night breath sweet.

God who dances with creation,
plants your likeness in the people,
strikes the world with thunder,
send us out to fill the world with love.

*Echoes a prayer from the World Council of Churches,
by Janet Morley.*

Peace to the land and all that grows on it.
Peace to the sea and all that swims in it.
Peace to the air and all that flies through it.
Peace to the night and all who sleep in it.

PRAYERS OF CREATION

Copyright © 2005 Ray Simpson
Original edition published in English under the title
PRAYERS OF CREATION by Kevin Mayhew Ltd,
Buxhall, England.
This edition copyright © Fortress Press 2019

All rights reserved. Except for brief quotations in critical articles or reviews, no part of this book may be reproduced in any manner without prior written permission from the publisher. Email copyright@augsburgfortress.org or write to Permissions, Fortress Press, PO Box 1209, Minneapolis, MN 55440-1209.

Cover image: Cover photo by ansonmiao from iStock Cover design: Emily Wyland

Print ISBN: 978-1-5064-5957-8

www.ingramcontent.com/pod-product-compliance
Lightning Source LLC
Chambersburg PA
CBHW052038070526
44584CB00020B/3155